IN THE SPACE BETWEEN

to Róisín

*lovely to meet you
and good luck with
all your writings!*

Gerry Boland

[signature]

IN THE SPACE BETWEEN

*Annaghmakerrig
9/1/17*

ARLEN
HOUSE

In the Space Between

is published in 2016 by
ARLEN HOUSE
42 Grange Abbey Road
Baldoyle
Dublin 13
Ireland
Phone/Fax: 353 86 8207617
Email: arlenhouse@gmail.com
arlenhouse.blogspot.com

Distributed internationally by
SYRACUSE UNIVERSITY PRESS
621 Skytop Road, Suite 110
Syracuse, NY 13244–5290
Phone: 315–443–5534/Fax: 315–443–5545
Email: supress@syr.edu

978–1–85132–133–9, paperback

Typesetting by Arlen House

Cover images by Derval Symes

CONTENTS

For Miriam

IN THE SPACE BETWEEN

CINEMATIC

It is like a scene from a French movie
except this is Grafton Street
on a wet winter Sunday
and when she turns and walks away
there is no Montmartre in the distance
no Eiffel Tower beyond the rooftops
there is only her as she fades out
into the crowd of disinterested extras
and him at the top of the street
a crushed Bogart look-a-like
paralysed with something that should
feel like remorse but doesn't.

He imagines the camera rising slowly
the audience in the aisles torn
between the fear of losing sight of her
in her quaint Parisian rain hat
scarlet above the glum throng
and the need to stay focussed on him
the tragic figure in this movie
rooted to his slab of pavement
mouth still partly, comically, open
the way it had opened and seized
when she threw in the towel
walked off into the crowd.

A NIGGLING DOUBT

the old house he had watched them grow up in
was being sold
someone he knew whose time they said had come
was seen out and about
making a brave and cheerful fight of it
someone else was told to chuck the fags
or else

he himself staggered
from one small sickness to another
spending sleepless nights in bed
passing days in a drowsy stupor on the sofa

he had achieved a purity of self-pity
that until now had managed to keep
the vilest of the hounds at bay

he would he guessed outlast the lot of them
though a niggling doubt haunts him tonight
that he may not see another day
he knows there is no substance to it
a crazy idea that's all

still
it feels a little like the writing of a suicide note
this last poem
though it most definitely isn't

which fails to explain
why he is on his knees
pleading for forgiveness
to anyone who might be listening

IN THE SPACE BETWEEN

the pillow wears the round indent of your absent head

you have walked out on me many times
always I was at the door waiting when

a long time later
you would come back

I have one foot on the grass
one on the carpet beside our bed

somewhere in the space between
is where I spend my nights

listening to the distant city exhaling
its citizens to the suburbs

to here
where we live

this morning I awoke in a warm bed
turned to inhale your sweet breath

took hold of your hand and squeezed it
opened my eyes to find myself alone

you read me like I read the clouds
but better

you know me as I know you
but better

you leave me as you always leave me

Early Days

in a cold room nearby
her clock has stopped

here the stove warms the air
that carries the deafening clamour
of her absence

the daylight draws him from his bed
guides his fragile frame to the window
from where he stares out
at the empty parking space

later on there'll be an attempt
to stem the rot
a splash of paint here and there
some windfall wood chopped
a spring clean
though it not yet Christmas

overall the place is holding up well
which may be more than will be said
for he who shuffles through these rooms
in these early days of his new life

he appears to be taking the strain
but there is a weariness to his movements
a slowness in his thoughts
that would have to make you wonder
how long this façade can go on
and when would be a good time

to call for back-up

WALLS

god knows he'd worked hard to get there
now he watches in dismay
as the walls come tumbling down
falling in on him
crushing him

he doesn't have the nous to say stop
catch his breath, regain his balance
make everything still for as long as is necessary
he is on the floor drowning
going under fast

his flaky structures had stood so long
surrounding him
protecting him
typical of him to forget
how fragile they were

there had been intimations
there usually are
a few false alarms
one close shave
that nearly did for him

he'd seen them off
with an extravagant flourish
that disguised the terror
perhaps he will this time
perhaps not

DILEMMA

there are things he needs to say
but he cannot find the words

he is a pressure cooker
about to blow

damage is being done
deep inside where it cannot be seen

he feels it there and there
and yes there too

on top of all this
there is the exhaustion

though he sleeps every night like a baby
it feels as if he hasn't slept for a year

if he lowers his head now
if he lets his forehead touch

the cool pine of the kitchen counter
there is perhaps a chance

a small chance
he will never wake up

such a simple act of surrender
may solve his dilemma for good

It Felt Like This

like shit
like a thousand hammers
hammering away behind his eyes
like a giant press
squeezing in on his head
like the end of the fucking world

it didn't feel remotely like
another rough day on the Gaza Strip
or any of the 4010 days
in Guantanamo
and it never once felt like
the moment after another car bomb

it felt pathetic now
not like the end of the world
closer to self-loathing
than any real pain
this was the moment
he decided to get better

which he did for a while

SADNESS

sadness comes to you
when you're not paying attention

it hits you from behind
like a stiff wind snagging your coat-tails

pulling at you
dragging you down

sadness is like an old dog who gets her teeth
into your ankle and will not let go

it likes nothing better
than to catch you off guard

is a mean beast in that way
and it's true what they say

it has a nasty streak beneath
the sorry sadness of itself

sadness is a royal bastard
in search of a convenient seat

to plonk its ruinous arse on
and spoil the fun

ANGELOU

we could live like this
one day at a time
the snow outside hardening again
the road a ski track
lined by silent, rigid trees
we are back in our warm house
loading logs into the stove
memory music reaching out to us
from another room

soon the evenings will lengthen
and this frozen capsule of time
will slot into place far behind
that long drive to Fontainebleu in '81
four of us in the car
spaced out on booze and eight-inch joints
rolled by the cool Canadian
whose name I have forgotten
feeling part of something communal and special

yet each one of us a prisoner
of our private wounded selves
yearning to be healed by none other
than the Belfast mystic himself
who cried out for *Angelou*
through the open window
into the starry night of our future
as he does again now
into our past

SHOW ME ANOTHER WAY TO LOVE

it seemed like a dream now:
the beekeeper's advice
the long drive into town
the exchange of cash for poison
his manly stance outside her house

early that cool June evening
when the wasps were settling in for the night
just a dozen late shift workers still abroad
making their homeward journey
across lush green summer country

he surprised himself
his capacity for killing was boundless
a frenzied whine haemorrhaging into the night
as they sought an escape from the Armageddon
from the killing machine he had become

back in his bed
his eardrums humming
his mind taunted by a question
that twists into a riddle and wriggles free
show me another way to love

A Flower you Planted

all that day I searched for
a last scent of meadowsweet

all that year my head ached
with bittersweet memories

today I came upon your orange calendula
healing balm to ease the pain

IN HIDING

she dials down from time to time
checking in

I am doing fine
he says

a lie that comes easily
so many years of practice

he will surface
a concession he knows must be made

and if the mood allows
he might stay a while

though she has learned
not to count on it

she waits
she will always wait

it is what she does best
so many years of practice

RED CLOCK

now that it's all settled
I can hear that red clock's second hand
edge relentlessly forward

all else is quiet
too quiet

the large unslept-in bed
invites no one in but the cold
a cold that finds its way
to where her icy feet lay in wait

over there, the old radio she never used
and here, above where I lie,
the mould on the walls encroaching still,
the odour of paint that never fades

there were other invisible things
that couldn't be kept at bay,
one in particular haunting every room
we lived in, even this one
where the red clock ticks and the light of the day
retreats into a deathly gloom

a cold silence creeps down my back
fastens me to the pale wall forever

WE WERE NOT DROWNING, SWEETHEART

we never saw you waving from the water's edge
we were immersed in another world
our heads like seals in the foam
our legs charged by the currents
our bodies electric under the sun
truly, we never saw you waving;
only the lifeguards as they ploughed towards us

BONFIRE

It was June
a good month for a bonfire.

She chose the first dry day
a day filled with fiery promise

cleared a path through the meadow
wheeled the loaded barrow

past buttercup and foxglove
and long grasses that brushed her bare legs.

His love poems got the blaze going
hundreds of them – earnest, naïve, lovesick

countless hours of angst gone up in seconds
in a great big whoosh of love.

Into the passion flames were tossed,
the usual metaphors, a thousand clichés

and a catalogue of political rants,
all dutifully dispatched and engulfed.

A container load of nature poems
kept the blaze going into late afternoon.

It was June
a good month for a bonfire

the poet's wife confided
to the stranger on the plane.

WHAT KIND OF LOVE?

The first time was the last time,
fin de soireé, Châtelet les Halles.

Do you laugh like that now?
Does your face still light up train carriages?

Do you still traverse that great city
late at night?

I cannot see you older
or changed in any way

though just now I may have imagined
your fifty-something self

chuckling with your grandchildren
in a small garden in the sun.

Mostly it is you at nineteen I see,
your eyes settled briefly on mine

as I stare at you across the tracks.

What kind of love is this
that lingers in a dark recess of my memory?

Why do you,
least known, *unknown*,

come to me so often,
like now, in this square room

reaching through the years
calling to me to cross the tracks
follow you home?

AND THIS IS TO FORGET YOU

put away your smile sweetheart
I'm like a moth to a flame
I'm not ready to fall in love
least of all with you smiling
now at this old man as he falls
towards you while remaining
perfectly still

you have given me a theme for the day
and you would be astonished
as I am
yet when you return tomorrow
with your bewitching tales
you may or may not notice
that I have gone

I caught a glimpse of you this morning
before you left
later I searched the wind and the sky
found you in the shadows of the lake
in the swifts that skimmed the grass
waited till the chill of evening
cooled my flaming heart

and this is to forget you
for forget you I must
your splendour has distorted everything
and I am old and disappointed enough
to recognize a pipe dream when I see it
lighting up whatever room
you happen to be in

SKELETONS

in August in my healing house
long lost friends broke the silence
they came with tiny reinforcements
four minds with a licence
to take this ordered space apart

with unrestrained energy and clamour
delving into nooks and crannies
innocents who knew no qualm
or fear of finding long forgotten
skeletons in cupboards

that night I watched them fall asleep
to tales of mother hubbards
and later still the adults sat
while four tots slept
and drained the bottles one by one

by midnight we had swept
under the carpet
that evening long ago
when only one of you had come
to say you had to go

NINETY SIX

it's a great age, I say
to which you scoff
don't make me laugh, you try it

you hadn't long to go
yet your gritty spirit tightened its grip
on the little you had left

you'd always chased the past
now it was all there was
the life you'd lived, relived over

each day you told me stories
some I knew
others I had forgotten

and one that wouldn't go away –
you on your black bicycle in 1937
freewheeling along the Featherbed

my mother merging with your shadow

A NEW DAY

one on top of another they come
each pushing the old one aside
with a brisk energetic shrug
bearing no malice as it cloaks itself
with the mantle of a new day

as with the others that have come and gone
today is determined to maintain momentum
and will not be deflected
by your futile reluctance
to let the old one go

ah yes, old man Yesterday
how casually you were shoved aside
by this upstart who wills you
even as you linger in a bedroom
where death has slid silently in

to embrace its fresh promise
turn your back on its older cousin
that you know
as you move away from the window
will shadow all the days of your future

SEPTEMBER

this is my last day of lounging around
a cool breeze has sliced through the cushion of summer
has made the meadow shudder

a pen records the dragonfly hypnotised at the iron gate
these dense brambles thick with blackberries
those dark clouds about to disrupt my small universe

down into the dying light falls an autumn rain
one single drop a cloudburst on the u of summer

time to circle the wagons
gather up my odds and ends

mosey indoors, rebuild my world

SOMETHING TO CHEW ON

we spent the day shitting
the term we used
for digging in cow dung
enriching the soil
giving the earth worms
something to chew on

it was pleasant work
extract of Freisian bowel
organic no less, buried
under black plastic for two months
the shit was deliciously pungent
sweet and perfumed and oddly exotic

we worked in tunnel seven
rain pelted the see-through cover
wind whipped at the open doors
some of the problems of our banjaxed nation
were forensically examined and casually solved
while the shit was dug in

Towards a Safe Mooring

and here you are in your garden
the long garden of your middle years
you are taking in or putting out the washing
one way or another you are at work
your default state in a house
that brought you to your knees
on which you now turn your back

you raised your children here
later they will wonder how you did it
how the burdens you carried went unseen
the small miracles you performed unnoticed
and now the task to trump the rest
the hauling single-handedly on steady shoulders
an entire family to a safe mooring

here you are then in your garden
taking in the washing one last time
the house overlooking it all
sensing in its hollow walls
some monumental change
the air itself alert to your grief
unsure of what the future will bring

now that it has lost its soul

The Far Side of the Hill

there were three of them
trapped inside the devious device
they were lured into
sometime in the small hours

an early morning drive delivered them
to the wood on the far side of the hill
a treacherous place
for small succulent mammals

they'll head for an old ruin
or if their run of luck continues
a warm house where an elderly bachelor
couldn't be bothered

last night's confinement
may have raised a tiny hair or two
yet will their unlikely release
in among the trees be any better

at the end of this November day
than the sudden spring of a trap
a bellyful of poison
a plaything for our murderous tabby?

let's not fool ourselves
with this feel-good baloney
the far side of the hill is a rambler's paradise
but it's no place to raise a family

BEYOND THE FARMYARD GATE

the signs are ominous
in flat fields near farmhouses
clouds of sheep have formed

yesterday dogs brought
five thousand down
the northern hills

they stand and wait
for whatever lies beyond
the farmyard gate

soon yesterday's panic will pale
amid the clamour and the chaos
the falling on the fouled ramp

the breathless cramming
in the semi-darkness
of the transport truck

CARGO

we're in the slipstream of your fear
a fear that fouls the wind tunnel
of these high hedges shadowing
mean northern roads

we shut the windows
the stench would turn a cast-iron gut –
worse, the sleeping child will wake
with questions we cannot answer

your journey has just begun
across endless motorways
and seas that dip and rise
to the camouflaged slaughterhouses

of Cairo and Metz and Gdansk –
there will be the usual welcoming party
as you stumble down the ramp
a greeting undreamed of

as you grazed the soft meadows
over dark northern bogs

CHRISTMAS EVE

sit down and have a rest
our work is almost done
circle the family wagons
all are safely home

tomorrow we will raise our glasses
toast the year past, the year ahead
slump on sofas with bloated stomachs
fall asleep with Marilyn in *Some Like It Hot*

turkey farms are silent now
slaughterhouse floors are drying out
and there
beneath a darkening hedgerow

a one-in-a-billion broiler
huddles alone and uneaten
a miraculous survivor
with a tall tale to tell

if the fox will listen
if the mink had a heart

THE PRIZE

there they are at baggage reclaim
seven middle-aged men in khaki
armed to the teeth with murderous paraphernalia

from a Marseilles *magazin de la chasse*
seven fur coats cluster nearby
a close-knit group of loyal warm wives

there'll be no blasting at the skies today
the birds are long asleep
but they'll be up first thing

unaware of plans
hatched over dinner
to leaden the morning air

the days pass badly for the men
cock-ups and mix-ups, not a gun fired for five days
the driver learns with muzzled amusement

he and his wives have been touring
to cliffs and rings
glass factories and blather castles

on the last morning the camera phones are busy
capturing the prize proudly laid out
on the blood-stained car park

while most were asleep, sparrows and crows
magpies and pigeons, a gull for God's sake –
rallies of dawn bullets, the gunmen content

SPRING LAMB

fluffballs in fields
we see them and soften

rejoice in their innocence
refuse to imagine

their exuberance silenced
on a slaughterhouse floor

FARMER

he is here in my head now
a hardy old buck leaning on the gate

as the truck pulls away and he waves farewell
with a tear in his eye

to his darling lambkins and sweetheart sheep
his cherished calves and good-as-gold cows

as their new life begins with their shit and piss
oozing through the truck's hosed-down floor

THE BUTCHER'S CLOCK

the clock in the local butcher's
never misses a beat

I see it sometimes as I pass
catch its outrageous denials

I'm a clock on a whitewashed wall
it ticks into my ear

there's no blood on my *hands*
it tocks

I quicken my step
to escape

the timeless lies,
the calculated claims of innocence

A PROBLEM WITH THE SPRING CLEANING

tell me this
how is a man to get the spring cleaning done
with every nook and cranny under occupation

the spring will be summer by the time I carefully
coax each frantic creature into this old jam jar
and deposit in some distant garden

I can see a time coming when like a devout Jain
I will haunt this tumbling-down house
a veil over my mouth and nostrils
thick socks on my feet
a soft brush in my hand to sweep
the near-invisible creatures from my cautious path
no longer daring to venture outside
where calamity is certain

and one other thing –
how many useless slugs are at this very moment
millimetering their way across my driveway

those intellectually-challenged lowlifes
have not the slightest conception of the inconvenience –
the fading light, the scouring of the grey gravel
the messy gathering of each and every delicacy –
they have no way of knowing that my clumsy caress
is a curious act of compassion
they'll resent my mauling fingers before take off
and soft landing in Malone's meadow

it will not I know curtail their mischievous malingering
they'll be back tomorrow night
same time same place

An Old Fly

such a rest you're having on my canvas shoe
a welcome change from the usual hullabaloo

are you slipping now into your funeral gown
or are you just an old fly slowing down

resting on my canvas shoe?
old flies have to rest too

Pheasant

we are wide awake
though had we been asleep
you would have woken us anyway
your inimitable shriek
shattering the silence of the morning
our ears alert and tracing
the swish of your large wings
down into the sleeping meadow

what disturbed you?
our neighbour's cat perhaps
who likes to mooch about here
just after dawn
or that fox we saw the other day
amble past the kitchen window
casually, in broad daylight
as if laying down a marker

perhaps it was that thug
who tied poor Jamsie to a chair
roughed him up
left him for dead
then popped next door to Mrs Wynne
removed her pension from her purse
split her lip with one hard slap
that shut the old bitch up

we should be listening
should we not
for the sound of footsteps
the cold chill of breaking glass
instead our ears are filled
with the whoosh of displaced air
the vacuum trailing the pheasant's
flight to safety

listen
sshh now
you can just about hear her moving through the meadow
quietly working her way through the long grass

THE WELL

a healer told her about the well
how the water was unlike no other
how people travelled for miles
it was that pure, that therapeutic

she put seven empty containers
in the boot of her car
drove nine miles along roads
that rested on Leitrim bog

found a queue of cars waiting
for the water, engines idling
like O'Connell Street it was –
she felt a rash coming on

the beginnings of a fever
and an anger brewing that she
knew could come to no good
in a place as wild as this

I live among amadáns
who don't see the connection
between a broken planet
and their own plain stupidity

she thought these thoughts
as she drove the nine miles
back the way she had come
in search of the good water

GOOD SAMARITAN

you swept by again today
a human hurricane
leaning into the wind

though your eyes were open
you did not see me
you never do

you remind me of a slender tree
tall and battered with deep roots
keeping you grounded

in your absence
I like to sit here
on the cold pavement

imagine you on your rounds
your briefcase filled
with miraculous intentions

if we ever speak
I will tell you something
that will surprise you

how you have the look
of a good Samaritan
in your charity shop suit

how I would follow you
obedient and loyal
across this sad city

for together I believe
we can heal the unhealthy
cure the incurable and –

why not
don't I have the inside track? –
home the homeless

please
whoever you are
sweep by me again soon

ISLAND

washed up on the sand
as in a dream
you wake to the smell of coconut
the pleasant heat of the sun

barefoot
the soft sand is hot on your soles
as you walk towards the palm trees
their shade

memory fails you
how you got here
where you came from
who you are

you step on the clean sheet of a new life
the torn and soiled sheets of your past
lost somewhere in the deep ocean
from which you have been reborn

you walk for most of that first day
help yourself to the fruit of paradise
beside a small stream you lie down
lower your face into the water

from the summit of the highest hill
you survey your island
begin to map out – already –
the eternal days of your future

MAGICIAN

like a magician he kept his cards up his sleeve
and like an illusionist he was unreadable

he lived in an exercise yard of the mind
bending occasionally to pick up a shard
of ancient pleasure, hold it up to the light

no one who knew him claimed to know him
beyond that smile he would let hang in the air
like a nineteenth-century levitator practicing his craft
before an awe-struck audience, only to deflate
their wonder in a neatly choreographed collapse

at such times
– his mischievous smile wrong-footing us –
we would be complete again
the rabbit back in the hat

once when we were abandoned for a year
the air that he left behind all but suffocated us –
his absence more poisonous than his presence
we breathed him in
spent poets walking towards the cliff face

we didn't know it then but he was the black cards
in the deck, who shuffled our small lives
as we played fearlessly aboard the wreck

WORDS

Just when you need them
they form a huddle inside,
coagulate, refuse to move.

There is no stopping them today,
they course through me
unable to contain themselves.

Unconcerned with originality
they operate according to their own rules
like gravity in reverse,

or the bowel forcing the waste upwards.
Words that have been entangled
separate,

regain their identity,
understand their purpose ,
rush gleefully to the surface.

And here they are
in all their finery,
in all their banality.

STRANGER

how did he become like this
a stranger no less
who grips her shoulders
purses his puffed-out lips
smothers her cheeks with sloppy kisses?

she feels no fondness, just fear
of what he has passed on to her
a stain as yet unseen
an unpleasantness she senses is already there
working its insidious way through her

where did he come from?
what monster sired him?
what vixen mothered him?
he stands out from the crowd
comes to her in her dreams

he will always be there
tormenting and belittling her
yet, oddly, a complete stranger –
if nothing else, and it is no small thing
she has managed to achieve that

BUTTERFLY

after a winter behind the sofa
it drops like a corpse
into the glass jar
warms its wings
under an April sun
and like Lazarus
rises into expectant air

for seven years
he has clipped her wings
held her captive
now would be a good time
to let in some light
stand back and watch
as she crawls out the door

BLACK SPOT

the beige linen suit
that felt hat
the pensive lean against the stone wall

he takes in the field
the foals the mares the stallions
every detail noted and absorbed

it is there is no denying
an idyllic pastoral scene
yet no one stops along this road

certainly not on this downhill bend
where last month a car came to grief
landing upside down in the field

the horses' uneventful lives unsettled
by a long-drawn-out tragedy
I can see him still

and I am miles away now
I suspect he is in mid composition
for there was a lyrical quality to his brow

as he surveyed the scene of the carnage

SANYINJIAO

my ninth session with the acupuncturist
and some sort of corner has been turned
that last needle did it
pressed into the point of convergence

san – yin – jiao

all three yin areas convulsing
my right leg in violent spasm
lifting off the plinth like a rocket
my bony knee connecting with her chin

and down she goes onto the carpeted floor
and out I go for the count
dreaming of three rivers of energy
coming together in uncommon harmony

she picks herself up
goes to greet the four-thirty client
chin tender
confidence soaring

THE LOCAL ACUPUNCTURIST

near the end it all got out of hand
a dried tea stain on the kitchen table
took on the image of a lonesome Panda
one-eyed, toothless, calling to her

she popped eight Chinese pills
pea-shooter size round black and shiny
five times a day and thought nothing of it
washed them down with weak green tea

one day she would look up from her bowl
and her Chinaman would be there
waiting patiently for her to finish
before they began the long trek to Lanzhou

she had she was certain
not a trace of Chinese blood in her
yet there was no denying her slow transformation
from Roscommon farming stock pure bog

only yesterday she spoke across the kitchen table
to John, husband of twenty-two years
are the potatoes cooked enough for you she asked
and her question twisted through the Rossie air

in a Chinese of perfect accent
impeccable pitch

MOONEY'S BAR

it was where she spent her days
she was the life and soul
of a party that never ended
a barstool with her name on it
her life going down the toilet

she comes to the café to forget
to be no one among the crowd
to nurture the life she has reclaimed
if only just

she orders an espresso
settles in to settling down
early Sunday morning
in the centre of town

an overweight buffoon she slept with once
crashes through her fragile calm
See you in Mooney's at noon he booms
into his fancy Samsung phone

she leaves a tenner on the table
descends to the street
for an early hit of retail therapy
that might, if the gods are on her side
disperse her rising panic

Rift

once they were as close as brothers
such impossible loyalty

now a studied avoidance is acted out
as they cross paths on a quiet street

a reach for a phone that hasn't rung
a one-way conversation into the ether

an offhand glance across the road
at someone who isn't there

a considered examination of the ground
as if all answers to all questions

were inscribed in small complex lettering
on the old grey pavement flagstones

and there they sit apart
in a downtown café

learned experts
at not noticing the other

what odd drama played out
to uncouple these two inseparables?

something intimate and intense no doubt
a tragic-comedy stubbornly overacted

leaving wounds that can never heal –
look at them

who would ever think that they were once
as close as brothers?

SECONDS AWAY ...

are these the rules then, man to man
we try to hurt the other as much as we can

it's an age-old game yet full of surprises
complexity dressed in elaborate disguises

it's patently clear that you are the brain
yet I am the expert in dishing out pain

friends again we walk away
we're both content we've had our say

until the next time when one of us
is out of line and there's a fuss

Christ there's nothing like a good old row
the adrenalin rush the Pow! Pow! Pow!

TO SILENCE

you are driving me insane
your dinner party views
your coffee shop opinions
your post office queue certainties

what makes you think
you can drone on like this
when it's clear that you are
clueless

I was like you once
held court on bar stools
let the world know where I stood
on this issue, on that –

let me raise my glass to silence
drink to those who have no answers
who muddle through their precious lives
without adding to the landfill

of endless, useless discourse

TOMORROW

a hazy start perhaps
fog slowly lifting
a new day unveiled
to silent applause

you might wake to rain
sweeping across the valley
or a landscape transformed
by a silent snowfall

in either case you will barely
notice the miraculous beauty
distracted as you usually are
by life's inconveniences

for some it will be a day
they will wish to forget
countless others will name it
the happiest of their lives

but for you
the highs the lows the mundane
all the things you took for granted
gone in a whisper

the day yesterday took on a new meaning
and tomorrow none at all

THE LAST WORD

here it comes
rushing onto the page regardless
the thrill of being on the move

each word a step into the unknown
thoughts pushed to the abyss
of a new line

words tumbling over themselves
in a frantic bid to be the sting in the tail
the last word in a punch line to die for

ACKNOWLEDGEMENTS

Acknowledgements are due to the editors of the following publications where some of the poems, or versions of them, first appeared: *The SHOp, Revival, MARGIE/Journal of American Poetry, Roscommon Herald, Ten Years in the Doghouse.*

'In the Space Between' was placed second in the 2012 Gregory O'Donoghue Competition and was subsequently published in *The Examiner*.

Thanks to Roscommon County Council Arts Office for residency bursaries at the Tyrone Guthrie Centre in Annaghmakerrig.

Thanks to the management and staff at Annaghmakerrig, for their warm hospitality, and for helping to make every visit a constructive and a memorable one.

Thanks to the members of the Moylurg Writers in Boyle for their support and encouragement down through the years.

Finally, a big thanks to my publisher, Alan Hayes.

Gerry Boland was born and lived for much of his life in Dublin and moved to north Roscommon in 1999. His first collection of poems, *Watching Clouds*, was published by Doghouse Books in 2011. In 2011 and 2012, O'Brien Press published his trilogy, *A Rather Remarkable Grizzly Bear*, the first of which, *Marco Moves In*, was nominated for an Irish Book Award. He has written two travel books on his native city, *A Pocket Guide to Dublin* (1994) and *Stroller's Guide to Dublin* (1999), both from Gill & Macmillan. His first collection of short stories, *The Far Side of Happiness*, is due out in 2016. He has been teaching creative writing in schools throughout the midlands and the northwest for many years.